FOOTBALL RISING STARS

ACCESS THE ACTION!

Scan the QR code to
hear this story for

FREE!

Published in the UK by Sweet Cherry Publishing Limited, 2025
Unit 4u18, The Book Brothers Business Park,
Tolwell Road, Leicester LE4 1BR, United Kingdom

Sweet Cherry Publishing Limited
Unit 31, The Pottery, Bakers Point,
Pottery Road, Dún Laoghaire,
Dublin A96 EV18, Ireland

2 4 6 8 10 9 7 5 3 1

ISBN: 978-1-80263-856-1

Football Rising Stars: Ona Batlle

Text by Luke Paton
Illustrations by Sophie Jones

www.sweetcherrypublishing.com

Printed and bound in Turkey

FSC www.fsc.org
MIX
Paper | Supporting responsible forestry
FSC® C221129

FOOTBALL RISING STARS

ONA BATLLE

THE UNOFFICIAL STORY

Written by

LUKE PATON

Sweet Cherry

CONTENTS

1

PLAYER OF THE MATCH

On the 2nd of November 2024, Barcelona's Ona Batlle lined up for a match against Eibar. The teams were playing in Liga F, the biggest and best league in Spanish women's football.

Barcelona was the greatest team in the league, and they wanted to win every match they played – and they often did.

Ona was only in her second season with the club, but she'd quickly taken on the same winning mentality as her teammates. As an attacking full-back, she knew it was up to her to stop the opposition from creating any scoring opportunities while also creating them for her own team.

The whistle blew for kick-off and Barcelona got the game underway. They outdid Eibar immediately, crafting a devastating attack in the first five minutes. It started when

Vicky López picked up the ball on the halfway line.

López passed it left to Clàudia Pina. As Pina drove towards the Eibar defenders in the middle of their half, Ona sprinted down the left-hand side and overtook the opposition's right-back. Pina spotted her run and slotted a perfectly weighted through ball into Ona's path.

Ona was in the penalty area as she approached the ball, tussling with the defender every step of the way. Ona got there first – just – as the defender dived in. The defender slammed into

Ona's right foot after she'd knocked the ball forward. She fell to the ground ... and the referee blew their whistle for a penalty!

Pina gave Ona a double high-five to congratulate her on winning the penalty, then they shared a quick chest-bump.

Moments later, Alexia Putellas knocked the penalty kick home and Barcelona were 1-0 up.

López made it 2-0 in the 21st minute, then Patri Guijarro

added a third goal in the 33rd minute. Barcelona were by far the better team, and Ona enjoyed spending a lot of the game defending her own goal.

In the second half, Ona hovered around the Eibar area. Aitana Bonmatí passed the ball to her, then Ona knocked it over to Putellas. Putellas found Mapi León way out on the left, so Ona wandered into the Eibar box. León cut inside to Bonmatí, who then passed the ball back to Putellas on the edge of the area. Ona was still in the box, and now she'd found two yards of space.

Putellas saw her and slipped her a lovely pass. An Eibar defender stretched for it, but she missed.

Ona took one touch, knocking the ball towards the six-yard box. She was in on goal with only the goalkeeper to beat. The angle wasn't great, and there was still an awful lot of work to do as the goalkeeper closed her down, but Ona didn't hesitate. She side-footed the ball between the goalkeeper and the near post. As it struck the back of the net, she felt

a rush of joy. *Goal!*

'An unlikely scorer but already her second of the season!' said the commentator. 'And didn't she take it well!'

Her teammates gave her high-fives and pats on the back as they crowded around to celebrate. They hadn't even been playing for an hour and were already 4-0 up!

It was exactly the kind of game Ona thrived in. She made dynamic runs all match, held her own in defence and even got on the

scoresheet. When the referee blew the final whistle, Ona won the Player of the Match award!

'Ona Batlle was the star of the show today,' said the commentator. 'Won a penalty and just played fantastically. But also, when it was needed, which wasn't too often, a good defensive cover as usual.'

Ona high-fived her teammates and opponents as she made her way off the pitch. It was a brilliant game, and her goal helped to keep Barcelona at the top of the Liga F table. She felt amazing. This was the reason why she loved playing for Barcelona.

It had been a long journey to get to this point, but she knew it had all been worth it...

2

EARLY DAYS

Ona Batlle Pascual was born on the 10th of June 1999. She lived in a town not far from Barcelona called Vilassar de Mar with her parents and older brother Joan. In fact, it was Joan who encouraged Ona to start playing football in the first place.

When Ona was really young, she

only liked doing one activity: rollerblading. She wanted to do nothing but rollerblade until she was six years old! It was only when she saw Joan playing football that she took up the sport.

Ona played football in the park with other boys and girls at first. Nobody ever wanted to play in goal, so everyone took their turn. Ona was a terrible goalkeeper, but she was awesome on the wing. It was immediately obvious that she had loads of talent.

Eventually, Ona started

to play for the local youth team. She played with the Vilassar de Mar side for one season, splitting her time between the boys' and girls' teams, and word soon began to spread about how good she was.

At the end of the season, while Ona was still only eleven years old, she got a call from Barcelona. They wanted her to try out for a spot in their academy, La Masia.

Barcelona was one of the biggest and most famous football clubs in the world, and the women's team were the most talented side in Spain's top league, Liga F. This was an incredible opportunity for someone as young as Ona. She had two training sessions with Barcelona, then they offered her a place on their youth teams!

The coaches knew Ona was a brilliant defender right away. Even though she was smaller than a lot of other players, she wasn't scared to get into tackles and was very hard to beat in one-on-one duels. She wasn't perfect, and sometimes she made mistakes, but the coaches believed she could be amazing in the future with their help.

La Masia is legendary for producing some of the world's greatest players. In the men's game, iconic Barcelona players such as Lionel Messi and Andrés Iniesta grew up there. In the women's game, Ballon d'Or winners such as Aitana Bonmatí and Alexia Putellas learnt to play there too. So Ona was definitely in the right place if she wanted to become one of the best football players ever!

The coaches at La Masia taught the youth teams how to play football the Barcelona way, which was in a style called tiki-taka. In tiki-taka football, the players kept possession by playing short passes to their teammates and constantly moving into space. The idea was that the team gradually worked the ball up the pitch, always keeping possession and finding the best passes through the opposition to create chances on goal.

Ona also learnt to play tiki-taka football in defence. When she was under pressure near her own goal, she never blindly blasted the ball as far away as possible. Instead, she always looked to pass her way out of trouble.

While she was still developing her game, Ona studied other full-backs. The person she looked up to most was the Brazilian player Dani Alves. She loved the way he moved up and down the wing, defending brilliantly but also helping his team in attack with crucial crosses. If she played like Alves when she grew up, she'd be very happy!

Ona played with the Barcelona youth teams for seven years, always hoping that she could break into the first team. But it slowly became clear to Ona that the club was spending lots of money buying big-name players, instead of using players from their youth teams. This meant she might never get the call-up she desperately wanted.

In the end, Ona made an important decision: she had to leave Barcelona. She didn't want to do it, but she had to if she wanted to play professionally someday.

I will work hard so that I can come back to Barcelona in the first team and play in a team that is strong enough to compete for everything, she thought.

So, in July 2017, Ona said goodbye to Barcelona and signed for Madrid CFF – a team that had just been promoted to Liga F. She was eighteen years old, and her footballing career was about to kick off.

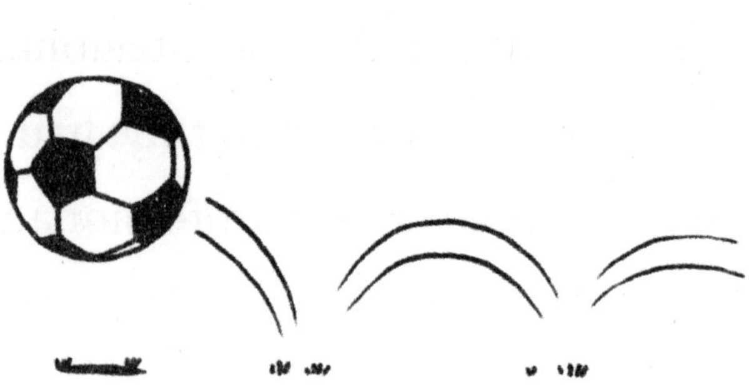

3

GROWING UP

Even though Ona had never played in Liga F for Barcelona or Madrid, she was already an experienced player for her country. She'd played for Spain's national youth teams at the Women's Under-17 Championships in 2015 and 2016, the 2016 Under-17 Women's World Cup and the 2017 Women's

Under-19 Championship. She'd even helped Spain win two of these tournaments!

So, when Madrid got promoted to Liga F, they were willing to take a chance on the eighteen-year-old Ona. She had loads of useful experience that could help them, and she was raring to go.

Ona accepted Madrid's offer right away and moved 600 kilometres away from home to join the club, leaving everyone and everything she knew and loved behind. It was a brave

decision, but it was a necessary one. If Ona wanted to grow as a player and compete in the top league, she had to do whatever it took.

Ona played for Madrid twenty-eight times in Liga F during her first season with the club. Getting minutes on the pitch was always the best way to develop in top-level football, so it felt amazing!

Soon enough, Ona's talent attracted the attention of another, bigger team in Liga F: Levante. She decided to sign up to the club in the summer of 2018, and it wasn't long before she made a big impression there too. A couple of weeks after her Levante debut in December 2018, Ona scored her first Liga F goal ever!

The goal came in a game against Logroño, scored in the 52nd minute. The achievement was made even sweeter because Levante won the game 2-4!

Ona earned a permanent place in the first team from that point on, making thirty-nine appearances in Liga F and scoring three goals in her first and second

seasons combined. That's pretty good for a defender!

Ona's standout performances with Levante also earned her a spot on Spain's first team! She made her debut in a friendly against Cameroon in May 2019, then she played in her first major tournament for the first team at the SheBelieves Cup in March 2020.

The competition was held in the USA – a country Ona had never been to before. It was so special to visit America for the first

time while representing her country! She was really excited and happy, but she was also very nervous. This was her first real chance to prove that she deserved to stay on the squad. After all, she was the youngest player there and didn't have as much experience as her teammates.

It's another dream come true, she thought. *I want to enjoy the experience to the fullest.*

Ona tried her hardest in training, always pushing herself to be the best she could be. Head coach Jorge Vilda noticed this and rewarded her with two starts during the tournament. The first was in a 3-1 win against Japan and the second was in a 1-0 defeat to the USA.

Spain finished the tournament as runners up with six points. Not everyone was satisfied with this, but Ona didn't mind. She felt like she was getting better with each and every new experience.

It's been a special year, she thought.

The year got even more special when Ona got an offer to join a new club: Manchester United (also known as the Red Devils).

Manchester United played in the Women's Super League (WSL) in England, and their manager, Casey Stoney, really liked how Ona played. She thought she was an exciting and fast full-back who fit perfectly with the club.

Ona had to think hard about joining Manchester United. Even though football players often move from club to club, it's rare for Spanish players in the women's game to leave their own country and play for different teams. If Ona joined Manchester United, she'd be stepping way out of her comfort zone. She'd have to be braver than ever.

But at the end of the day, the pull and legendary status of Manchester United was too much to resist. It was an opportunity Ona couldn't turn down.

'It's an honour and a pleasure to sign for Manchester United,' she said. 'I can't wait to meet my new teammates and help to contribute to as much success as I can.'

4

WELCOME TO MANCHESTER

The moment Ona stepped off the plane in Manchester, she realised how big of a decision she'd made. She was only twenty years old and had moved to a country where she didn't speak the language! It was really scary. Had she made a terrible mistake?

What am I doing with my life? she thought.

It didn't help that England was in lockdown to stop the COVID-19 virus from spreading at the time. The UK government had told everybody to stay home and not visit family or friends as a safety measure to stop people from getting infected, but it made adjusting to life in a new country very hard for Ona. She spent a lot of time crying because she didn't have any friends or family nearby. Ona couldn't go back home to Spain, and now she couldn't even explore

Manchester because many places were closed.

Manchester United manager Stoney didn't let any of the team hang out together when they weren't at training or playing matches. This was so they didn't break any government rules or end up getting sick. But that didn't leave a lot of things left for Ona to do!

One day during the lockdown, Ona felt very low. She was almost 2,000 kilometres away from home with no way of getting back, and it had become too much for her to handle. She spoke to a mental health expert at the club and ended up crying her eyes out. She found it all so tough. But in a strange way, it was good to get the crying out of her system!

Despite all of this, Ona never thought about leaving Manchester United. She just kept reminding herself why she'd moved there in the first place.

'I'm a really independent person,' she told herself. 'I've always wanted to improve and grow up as a person.

When you leave your country, that's when you must grow up.'

Manchester United did everything they could to help Ona settle in. They gave her a translator who went to team meetings, training sessions and matches with her, so Ona knew what was going on while she was learning to speak English. That was great, but it also had its downsides.

In December 2020, for example, Manchester United played an away game against Reading. Manchester United won the game 1-2, but Stoney was screaming instructions at Ona from the sidelines in the last minute. Ona heard Stoney but didn't understand any of it, so her translator started screaming the same instructions in Spanish. Having two people screaming at her was way too much to take in at once!

Thankfully, things slowly started to change. Ona's English kept getting better, and she even began to understand the Manchester accent. After talking to Manchester United players such as Ella Toone and Millie

Turner, Ona started saying words you'd never learn in a language lesson, such as 'innit'!

Eventually, the lockdown restrictions lifted and Ona was able to explore the country with other players.

On New Year's Day in 2021, she went to visit a lake with Everton player Damaris Egurrola. Even though the lake was freezing cold, Egurrola suggested that they should have a splash anyway. Ona *was* looking for things to do that she thought might be fun, so she ended up getting into the water. She'd never been in water so cold in her entire life, but it was definitely fun!

Ona was living with Ivana Fuso, who played as a forward for Manchester United at the time. They had some great times together too, but Ona often explored England on her own. She drove to other cities such as Liverpool, York and Chester. She even went as far as Newcastle – on the other side of the country – just so she could see it!

Although Ona liked living in England, the thing she missed most about living in Spain was seeing the sun. Compared to Spain, Manchester was very grey for much of the year!

So when she saw a glimpse of the sun one day, Ona got in the car and drove to a beach in Formby. She planned to sit on the sand, read her book and enjoy the sun... But by the time she got there, it started to rain! It was also really windy. She was only on the beach for fifteen minutes before she gave up and drove back home.

While Ona felt like it took her a long time to settle into the team,

Manchester United fans had no idea. After all, she played absolutely brilliantly for the Red Devils from the first moment she joined.

5

A GREAT START

After Ona signed for Manchester United, she said, 'I've been waiting a long time for this. I am looking forward to getting started with my new team, developing myself as a player and achieving great things with this club.'

Ona made her debut in the first game of the 2020/2021 WSL season. Manchester United was playing against Chelsea, and it seemed like Ona and forward Leah Galton were going to make a great combination straight away. They caused Chelsea lots of problems on the left-hand side and helped their team keep a 1-1 tie.

After beating Birmingham City and Brighton & Hove Albion in the next two games, Ona and her teammates stumbled and lost to Liverpool

in the third – but they quickly got back on track with victories over Tottenham Hotspur and West Ham United. They then achieved an impressive 1-0 over one of the strongest sides in the league, Arsenal. That win gave them three points and sent them to the top of the WSL table!

'I'm proud of the character and ambition of my team and this great club,' said Ona. 'It is my desire to continue working with them.'

Ona played nineteen times in the WSL that season. While her team couldn't hold onto the number one spot, they did manage to finish the league in fourth place – one point behind Arsenal in third.

Ona had many standout moments throughout the season, one of which came in a game against Chelsea. After chasing down Chelsea's Fran Kirby for half the length of the pitch, Ona shouldered her off the ball and then calmly passed it to a teammate. She also made runs up and down the left wing, rounding defenders and looking for teammates in dangerous positions.

Ona made another important challenge in a match against Arsenal, flicking the ball away in the penalty box to deny Beth Mead a shot on goal. Her defensive tactics were amazing!

In other games, Ona made use of her attacking skills. She recorded several assists, giving her teammates golden opportunities to belt the ball home.

Ona didn't score a goal for herself, but she did win a very important prize for her efforts. At the end of the 2020/2021 season, she was voted as Manchester United Women's Player of the Year. What a way to finish her first year in English football!

Ahead of the 2021/2022 season,

Manchester United switched managers from Casey Stoney to Marc Skinner. Ona was eager to show Skinner what she could do, so she jumped right into her second year with the club and performed incredibly in their opening game against Reading. There was no stopping her once she got into a flow, and she had one of her best moments yet…

Manchester United were already 1-0 up when Ona got the ball on the left wing in the second half and

passed it inside to Ella Toone, who was on the corner of Reading's box. Toone turned to face the goal and then cut the ball back to Ona, who'd darted into the area. Ona took one touch to control it and then, with little back lift, smashed the ball towards the top corner of Reading's goal. The goalkeeper didn't stand a chance. It rattled the back of the net!

'The hit is in magnificently!' screamed the commentator. 'Ona Batlle with a beauty!'

It was the first goal she'd ever

scored for Manchester United!

Ona spread her arms in joy as the rest of her team hugged her and slapped her back. What a rush!

Ona scored her second Manchester United goal in a League Cup tie against Manchester City in November 2021. The match was poised at 1-1 when Galton gave the ball to Ona on the left-hand side. Ona raced past Manchester City's Ruby Mace then squared the ball to her teammate Alessia Russo, who was right on the penalty spot. Russo side-footed a shot that the goalkeeper palmed away. Ona charged towards the loose ball, but City's Demi Stokes got there first.

I have to go hard to her, thought Ona.

Stokes thought she had more time to clear the ball, but Ona was on her now. She shoulder-barged Stokes off the ball, turned quickly and fired a left-footed shot into the back of the net. *Goal!*

All of Ona's performances that season were amazing, and she hoped they were enough to get Manchester United into the Champions League – a competition between the very best teams in Europe. Ona had always wanted to play in the tournament.

Unfortunately, the Red Devils didn't quite get there in the 2021/2022 season. They finished in fourth position again – one place out of the qualifying spots – but Ona was determined to try again next season. She wasn't finished winning games and scoring goals in a Manchester United shirt yet!

6

GLORY, GLORY, MAN UNITED

The best goal Ona scored for Manchester United came in a WSL tie against Aston Villa on the 3rd of December 2022.

Ona started a move deep in the Villa

half, passing the ball wide to the right. She spotted a big hole in the Villa defence between the full-back and the centre-back and wandered into the space, pointing in front of her to tell her teammates where she wanted the ball next – and that's exactly where she got it.

Ona controlled the ball inside the Villa box, a little on the right. This was usually when she'd cross the ball to another player, but this time she tried something different.

I'm going to shoot, she thought.

Ona knew it was a really good strike the moment she struck the ball. It rocketed through the

goalkeeper's hands, blasted off the bar, hit the far post and bounced into the net. The goal was even more special because it was part of a massive 5-0 win at Old Trafford, the home of Manchester United and one of the best stadiums in England!

Ona put in another sparkling performance in an FA Cup quarter-final match against Lewes.

In the 8th minute, Maya Le Tissier sent Ona free down the right-hand side with the ball. Ona ran at the Lewes defence before putting a low cross into Russo in the box. Russo's presence was enough to cause a Lewes defender to lose her cool and accidentally kick the ball into her own net.

Lewes made it 1-1 in the second half, but the tie didn't last long.

Five minutes after the equaliser, Toone found Ona in loads of space on the edge of the Lewes area. As the ball rolled towards her, Ona realised she didn't have time to control it. She saw that two or three of her teammates were in great positions in the box and knew that any hesitation would give the defenders a chance to recover. Instead of waiting, she put in a strong first-time cross. It was pinpoint accurate, allowing Vilde Bøe Risa to simply nod it home.

A third goal from Nikita Parris in the 89th minute secured the win, putting Manchester United through to the next round.

The game against Lewes was one of Ona's best yet, and her manager, Skinner, was very impressed with how freely she played.

When Ona had first arrived at the club, she'd been playing the tiki-taka way she'd been taught in Spain – short passes to gradually work the ball up the pitch. This was very different to most WSL players, who preferred to run with the ball for longer, so she'd been working on adapting to match their style. The more she practised running at defenders and dribbling with the ball, the more she enjoyed it. She also worked on her crossing in training. If she was going to be an attacking full-back, she knew she needed a brilliant cross to add the finishing touch to her electrifying runs.

In the FA Cup semi-final against Brighton & Hove Albion, Ona put all of those skills together on the pitch. At half-time, Skinner told the team to drive at Brighton because they were playing narrow, giving his players the chance to run the ball down the wings. So, as soon as the game restarted and Ona got the ball, she thought, *Well, I'm going to just start to drive.*

She skipped past one player then kept going and going until she reached the byline. At the last moment, she knocked a solid pass into the middle – and Galton slotted it into the net!

Manchester United went on to beat Brighton 3-2, booking their place in the FA Cup final at Wembley Stadium! It was the first time Ona and the Manchester

United women had played at this magnificent stadium, and it was a day to remember. Even though the team eventually lost to Chelsea 1-0, Ona loved the game. Over 77,000 fans were watching, all screaming for their teams to win. It made for an incredible atmosphere.

'It's so special to be a Man United player,' said Ona. 'The fans are so loud you can almost feel them when you're out on the pitch. I think it's one of the most special things that I will take from my time in Manchester – the people.'

Manchester United finished the 2022/2023 season in second place in the WSL and as runners up in the FA Cup. It was their best season ever... But it was the last one Ona competed in as a Manchester United player.

After three years in the WSL, she'd decided that it was time to go on a new journey with another club. 'I will always be proud to say that I was a Red Devil. Once red, always red,' she said.

However, she had a very important competition to deal with first.

7

NATIONAL CRISIS

During her last season with Manchester United, Ona was also busy making a new name for herself with Spain. She loved playing for her country, but something felt wrong in 2022.

The Spanish team was full of some

of the most talented footballers in the world. That includes amazing players such as Ona, Aitana Bonmatí, Olga Carmona, Alexia Putellas – the list goes on. So how come Spain weren't winning any major tournaments?

Spain's head coach, Jorge Vilda, had been in charge since 2015, but in all that time, Spain had been sent home in the first round of the knock-out stages of the 2017 Euros, 2019 World Cup and 2022 Euros. It was a frustrating run of results. But worse than all of this was the atmosphere within the Spanish squad.

Many of the players didn't feel like the team's technical staff or the Spanish football federation (RFEF) took them seriously. For example, they didn't think that the team were given enough time to prepare properly for important games. They also didn't like how other teams – including Spain's men's team – took planes to travel long distances, yet the women's team had to take a bus for the same journey. And, worst of all, the players didn't trust their coaches. Ona and fourteen other players from the Spanish national team decided they had to take a stand. They first met with the RFEF to make their concerns official. They said that the national team setup had to change or else the team would never be able to win a major tournament.

But after the meeting, the players felt like nothing was going to change, so they sent a strongly worded email to the RFEF saying that they didn't want to play for Spain until their concerns were taken seriously.

'I currently do not see myself in

a position to be a player eligible for selection for our national team and for this reason, I request not to be called up until the situation is reversed,' they wrote at the end of the email, which was sent in September 2022.

This was a very big deal! Ona loved her country and wanted nothing more than to win a tournament with Spain, but it was important to her to speak out against anything she didn't think was right.

Unfortunately, the email caused a split in the Spanish team. The public supported the women and applauded their bravery in speaking up. However, the RFEF showed their support for Vilda and his behind-the-scenes staff. The situation was very tense for a very long time.

The players who sent the email had lots of meetings with the RFEF and Vilda to find ways to work together in the future. The RFEF eventually promised to hire more people to help the players better prepare, physically and mentally, for their matches. They also said the team would fly more, stay in better hotels and travel to matches earlier to give them more time to get used to new environments.

Most importantly, the players felt like the RFEF had listened to their concerns about the atmosphere inside the camp. Ona and the others spoke to players who had carried on playing for Spain and discovered that things were getting better.

Not all of the players were 100% happy, even after six months of talking and negotiating, but Ona and seven others felt like the RFEF was finally on their side. They decided to make themselves available to rejoin the Spanish team in June 2023, right before the World Cup.

Of these eight players, only three were selected for Spain's 2023 World Cup squad: Ona, Aitana Bonmatí and Mariona Caldentey. The mood in the camp wasn't solved overnight, but the squad began to feel more like a real team. The months of tough conversations had been worth it.

The World Cup was hosted by Australia and New Zealand that year, so the team had to go on a tiring thirty-hour journey from Spain to

Auckland, New Zealand. They also had to get used to a time zone that was ten hours ahead of Spain, so they flew there ten days before they played their first World Cup game.

Ona had really bad jet lag when they arrived, which is when you have trouble sleeping while your body gets used to a new time zone. It was a weird feeling for Ona because she'd never had jet lag before. But after a few days, she got used to it.

Ona knew how lucky she was to play in a World Cup on the other side of the world. And even though the team had disagreed in the past, they all had one thing in common.

'We are all professional footballers,' said Ona. 'We know what we're here for. We all have the same goal: to win the World Cup.'

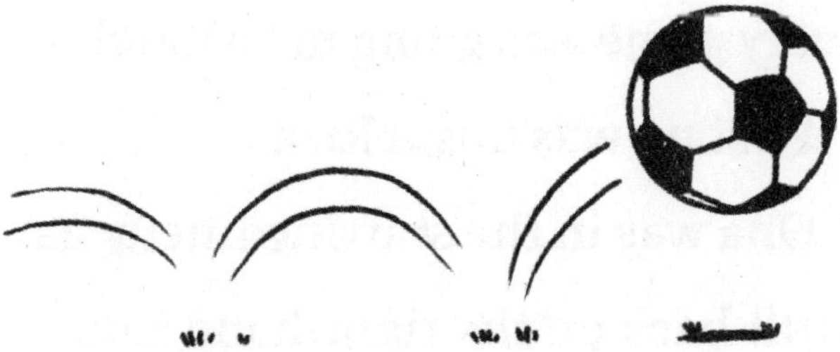

8

THE WORLD CUP

In the first stage of the 2023 World Cup, Spain were drawn in a group with Japan, Costa Rica and Zambia. Every game was going to be tough.

First up was Costa Rica.

Ona was in the starting lineup as a full-back on the right-hand side.

She knew her job was to defend well and give Spain attacking options by powering forwards whenever possible. Costa Rica were a strong team, but her time playing in the WSL had made her physically stronger too. She was ready for the challenge.

Ona's best moment in the game came about twenty minutes into the match when Spain were already 1-0 up. She got the ball on the edge of the Costa Rican area, passed it wide, then tried to find space in

the box. The ball eventually fell to her and she immediately squared it inside to Bonmatí, who was hovering unmarked by the penalty spot. Bonmatí controlled it skilfully, took one defender out of the game and then curled the ball into the bottom corner. It was a wonderful goal!

Ona almost set up another goal five minutes later when her perfectly weighted cross picked out Esther González, but her header was neatly blocked by the Costa Rican goalkeeper.

Despite that miss, Spain won 3-0 and moved on to the second group game against Zambia.

This match marked the first time Spain and Zambia had ever faced each other, and Ona was quite worried about playing against them.

'They have players who can surprise you on any counter-attack,' she explained.

As it turned out, Ona didn't need to worry. Spain easily beat Zambia 5-0 and qualified for the next round.

The team she should've been worried about was their next opponent… Japan.

Spain needed to defeat Japan to finish at the top of the group. However, the Japanese team ripped through the strong Spanish defence time and again to end on a score of 4-0.

This was a shocking defeat for Spain. But in a weird way, it was a good thing. That defeat only strengthened Spain's determination to do better in the knock-out stages.

'We have not seen the best of the Spain team and

I'm sure against Switzerland we will react positively,' head coach Vilda said. 'The team is together and in a few days we have to play a round of 16 game.'

Ona took inspiration from other top players in the squad, such as Alexia Putellas, Aitana Bonmatí and Salma Paralluelo. 'You know they are going to make you better,' she said. 'The ambition to win and be the best team in the world is something that is contagious.'

Spain certainly showed how good they were when they played against

Switzerland in the round of 16. They quickly broke down the Swiss defence and went on to win 5-1, with Ona playing her part in the second goal. She showed great instinctive play to win the ball from Switzerland and deliver a splendid cross into the box. A Spanish head flicked it on, then Alba Redondo headed it home. The team made reaching the quarter-final of a World Cup look easy!

But there were no easy matches from this point on. The quarter-final match against the Netherlands was the toughest one by far.

9

ROAD TO THE FINAL

Spain's quarter-final opponent, the Netherlands, had played extremely well in the 2023 World Cup, and they proved very hard to beat. Spain knew it would take a special moment to get them through to the next round.

During the match, Ona and Spain

tried their hardest to break through the Netherlands, but they didn't make a single chance for eighty minutes. It seemed like it was destined to be a goalless draw, until Spain managed to create one of the most breathtaking finishes in the whole tournament.

Spain scored a penalty in the 81st minute to make it 1-0, but then the Netherlands drew level ten minutes later to force the game into extra time.

Finally, just when it felt like it was going to penalties,

Paralluelo skilfully beat a defender and smashed the ball off the post into the back of the net. This goal put Spain through to the semi-final!

Ona was pleased with how she'd played in the matches so far. She hadn't scored a goal or recorded the most assists, but she had been excellent for her team throughout. One achievement she was particularly proud of was that she'd put more crosses into the box than any other player so far in the competition. Spain would need that kind of forward play when they came up against Sweden in the semi-final.

Neither Spain nor Sweden's women's teams had ever reached a World Cup final before, which meant there was a lot of pressure on both sets of players. Everybody on that pitch – and everybody watching at home – wanted to win and make history!

There was even more late drama in this game than there was in the Netherlands match. Spain went ahead with only ten minutes left to play through a sharp strike from Paralluelo, only for Sweden to pull level with a stunning strike in the last two minutes.

Despite this, Spain didn't let their heads drop. Instead, it took just one minute for Olga Carmona to score one of the goals of the tournament. As soon as Ona saw Carmona's blistering shot rebound off the bar and in, she raised her hands to the sky in celebration. She knew what it meant: her team were in the World Cup final for the first time ever!

Ona's parents had flown to Sydney in Australia to watch Ona compete in the semi-final, but they had to fly back to Spain because of work straight afterwards.

However, once they got home, Ona's mother desperately wanted to go back again to watch Ona play in the final. 'We have to be there if she has the chance of winning the World Cup,' she told Ona's father.

Ona's father wasn't so sure at first. After all, it was a twenty-hour flight from Spain to Australia. But how many chances would he get to see his daughter compete in a World Cup? In the end, they both flew back in time for the final.

Ona was glad they did. Spain's victory against Sweden meant they had a date with England to battle it out for the World Cup trophy. She was going to face many of the players she'd spent the last three years playing with in the WSL!

It's beautiful we shared three years together and now we're going to share a World Cup final, thought Ona.

It would be nice to see everybody again... But make no mistake about it, Ona and Spain were there to win the World Cup.

10

SPAIN ON TOP

'It's the game of their lives,' said the commentator as Spain and England walked out on the pitch on the 20th of August 2023. Neither team had won the World Cup before, so a new name would be etched on the trophy at the end of the match. But was it going to be England's or Spain's?

The game started at a fast pace. Ona attempted a shot on goal in the 4th minute that was blocked by Millie Bright. She also sent a cross into Paralluelo in a dangerous position in the 16th minute, but England were able to clear it away.

Both teams had excellent chances to open the scoring in the first twenty minutes. England hit the bar when Lauren Hemp's side-foot shot was inches too high, and Spain's Redondo had her shot saved by Mary

Earps at the other end.

It's going to be tough to score against her, thought Ona. She'd played with Earps for three years and knew the goalkeeper was in top form.

In the 29th minute, Spain won the ball off Lucy Bronze and began a fast counter-attack. Teresa Abelleira swept it wide to Mariona Caldentey. Caldentey held it while Olga Carmona, the team's captain, sprinted past her, then she played Carmona in behind the England defence. Carmona smashed the ball low and hard, and it shot past Earps's glove and flew into the corner of the net. It was 1-0 to Spain!

The Spanish players ran over to Carmona to celebrate and hug one another. What a moment! Ona was especially happy to see Carmona score. She knew how amazing she was and thought she was a great captain.

Ona played her part by defending well against England's Lauren Hemp and Rachel Daly. She was constantly tackling, blocking them from making good runs and passes. England shut

Ona's play down as well, but she did find a way through their backline close to the half-time whistle.

Ona drove at the defenders and reached the England box. Instead of going outside like she usually did, Ona cut inside and knocked a strong pass in towards the penalty spot. Paralluelo was there, as always, and clipped the ball neatly towards goal. It was past Earps before she even dived ... but it struck the wrong side of the post and went out for a goal kick.

Spain held onto the lead into half-time

and beyond. Ona had her hands full trying to keep Hemp quiet, and the only time Hemp managed to get past her she had a golden chance on goal. Thankfully, Hemp blasted it wide. Even when it looked like England might come back after Spain missed a penalty, the players remained calm. They carried on playing football their way and kept England at bay.

Ona had a chance to seal the game in injury time when Bonmatí played a perfect pass through the defenders.

Ona raced towards the England goal and took a shot, but it deflected off an England defender and Earps got down well to save it.

The last few minutes of the game passed agonisingly slowly. Finally, the referee blew their whistle and Spain were crowned as the world champions! As the Spanish players dived on top of one another, the celebrations from the Spanish fans in the stadium were wild!

Each player was given a World Cup winner's medal and a Spanish shirt with a star on it. The team climbed the podium together and lifted the World Cup trophy while fireworks exploded behind them. It was an absolutely incredible moment!

Through all the dizzying celebrations, Ona never forgot that some things were bigger than football. She spotted Lucy Bronze on her own on the England bench, clearly upset about what had happened on the pitch. Instead of ignoring her and carrying on enjoying her victory, Ona took the time to go over and comfort her friend and club teammate.

A photographer took a picture of Ona with her arm around a crying Bronze, and the picture warmed people's hearts all over the world. Two players from opposite teams put their loyalties to their countries to the side to show the true meaning of sportsmanship.

It was a very special ending to a very special day.

11

LIGA F

After the World Cup victory, some of the Spanish players enjoyed a holiday in Ibiza together. But after that blissful trip, Ona had a new challenge to face: life with a new club in a new league.

But this wasn't just any club. Ona had decided to go back home to Barcelona and play in Liga F!

'It has always been my dream,' she said. 'I'm really excited about sharing experiences with the rest of the squad.'

Ona had grown both as a person and a player since leaving Barcelona's academy at the age of eighteen. Not only had she played in a physically demanding league in the WSL, but she'd also fended for herself in a new country. She'd even travelled the world with the national team and won a World Cup! Now she was ready to apply everything she'd learnt to her new club.

In a strange twist of fate, Ona made her competitive debut at Barcelona in a September 2023 match against another former club, Madrid. Barcelona went 0-1 up in the first half after Caroline Graham Hansen found the net, then Ona got the ball wide on the left in the 84th minute. She dribbled around one player, past a second. She raced into the box, chased by a Madrid defender,

and smashed the ball into the box – right to the feet of her teammate, Asisat Oshoala. All Oshoala had to do was tap it into the goal, scoring Barcelona's second goal of the game. Ona was very happy to make a brilliant assist in her first game!

She only had to wait a little longer before she scored her first goal for the club. It came in an October match against Granada – and it was a screamer!

Ona started the move out on the left, playing the ball down the wing for

Paralluelo. Paralluelo controlled it, turned, then passed it inside for Ona to run onto. After taking one touch to move the ball out of her feet, Ona placed a perfect curling shot into the bottom corner. What a goal!

As soon as the ball hit the net, Ona wrapped her arms around Paralluelo and Paralluelo lifted her off the ground. The rest of the team ran straight over to congratulate her too.

Ona added two more goals in the 2023/2024 Liga F season. Her second one was a cheeky poke into the net

in the final minutes of an 8-0 victory over Madrid. Her third was a lovely side-footed finish after Bonmatí squared the ball to her in the box. It was the last goal of a 7-0 win against Athletic Club.

Barcelona played thirty Liga F games, winning twenty-nine and drawing one. It was a truly dominant performance that saw them win the league for the fifth season in a row. They added that trophy to the Supercopa de España Femenina trophy they'd won earlier in the year.

This meant Barcelona had the chance to complete a domestic treble, which when one team wins three competitions in the same season. All they had to do now was beat Real Sociedad in the Copa de la Reina final…

The final was played on the 18th of May 2024, and it was a great day for Ona! In the opening five minutes, she was played in behind the Real Sociedad defence, darted into the box and played a low cross to the Barcelona players streaming into

the area. It was blocked ... then rebounded right into her path again. Wasting no time, Ona blasted the ball at the Real Sociedad goalkeeper – and it was too hot to handle. *Goal!*

It was the perfect start, and Barcelona carried on scoring after that. Paralluelo and Graham Hansen made it 4-0 before Ona got on the scoresheet again. This time, Caldentey played a sweet pass through the defence and put Ona through on goal. She used her weaker left foot to delicately dink the ball past the goalkeeper and into the far corner. It was a beautiful strike!

Barcelona won the match 8-0, securing the domestic treble as well as the Copa de la Reina trophy. It was an incredible achievement, but Barcelona wanted more. If this was going to be a truly memorable season, they had to win a continental quadruple. This is when one team wins *four* trophies in one season, including one international trophy.

This meant one thing: they had to win the Champions League.

12

CHAMPIONS LEAGUE FOOTBALL

Ona had dreamt of playing in the Champions League ever since she started playing football. Now that she was with Barcelona, she'd finally got her shot to live that dream – and she wasn't going to throw it away. This was her chance to play against some of the best clubs in Europe, both at home and away in other countries.

Barcelona were drawn in a group with the Portuguese team Benfica, the German team Eintracht Frankfurt and the Swedish team Rosengård. These were the best teams in their leagues, and they were all difficult games for Barcelona.

Ona played a great game against Eintracht Frankfurt in the away match in November 2023.

Barcelona were 1-0 down when Caldentey passed her the ball on the left wing. Ona dribbled down the sideline, drawing the defender close to her. Then, when she realised the defender was going to try and tackle her, she found a burst of speed and zipped past her.

Now that she was almost on the byline in the Frankfurt box, Ona looked up and saw her teammate, Paralluelo, in space in the middle. She squared the ball into Paralluelo's feet, making it an easy goal for her. All Paralluelo had to do was knock it into the net, which she did. This got Barcelona back in the game, and they went on to win 1-3.

Ona and Paralluelo teamed up again in the away clash with Rosengård in December 2023. This time, Keira Walsh played Ona in behind the defence and Ona pulled it back for Paralluelo to drive it home.

Paralluelo celebrated by giving Ona a high-five and a hug. Barcelona ended up winning the game 0-6!

The pair did almost exactly the same thing

against Rosengård in the home leg. This time, though, Ona put in a pinpoint cross that swept behind the Rosengård defenders and right onto the left boot of Paralluelo. They were a thorn in Rosengård's side! Barcelona won again 7-0!

Those performances and goals were enough to help Barcelona top their group and go through to the knock-out stage. Their quarter-final opponent was the Norwegian team Brann, but Barcelona proved too strong for them. They beat Brann 1-2 in the first leg and 3-1 in the second leg, winning with a combined score of 5-2. But Ona knew better than anyone else that the semi-final was going to be much closer, as they were playing against the English WSL champions, Chelsea.

Ona slowly realised that Champions League football was especially hard for Barcelona because they were so dominant in Liga F.

Constantly winning matches meant they weren't being challenged enough, leaving them unprepared when they faced stronger teams such as Chelsea.

Perhaps that's why Barcelona weren't up to their best when they played against Chelsea in the first leg of the semi-final at the Olympic Stadium in Barcelona...

Barcelona had 54% of the possession, but they couldn't find a way through Chelsea's defence. Chelsea carried out their own game plan perfectly and won 0-1, thanks to a sensational strike from Erin Cuthbert.

'Barcelona have been stunned by a wonderful finish!' screamed the commentator.

It was the first time Barcelona had lost at their home ground since 2019, but that was how tough the Champions League was.

'If you're not at your best in the Champions League, you're not going to win,' said Ona.

If Barcelona wanted to get to the

final, they'd have to play a lot better in the away leg. Or was the continental quadruple one step too far?

13

SECOND CHANCE

The second leg of Barcelona's Champions League semi-final against Chelsea was played at Stamford Bridge stadium in London.

Before the match, Ona told herself that this match wouldn't be like the last one.

We know we can win this, she thought.

Ona had a big game and kept Chelsea's Johanna Rytting Kaneryd quiet on the right. She sneaked down the wing whenever she could and even managed a decent shot that was saved by the Chelsea's goalkeeper, Hannah Hampton.

Bonmatí eventually opened the scoring with a deflected shot that beat the goalkeeper, then Fridolina Rolfö doubled the score from the penalty spot. The team claimed a 0-2 victory on the night, winning the

semi-final with a combined score of 2-1. Barcelona were going to the Champions League final!

'This is why I came back to Barcelona,' said Ona. 'To play at this level and in the final of the Champions League. To do it for the club I've grown up supporting is like a dream.'

The final was against the French side Lyon.

Barcelona had played against Lyon in the Champions League final in 2019

and 2022, and Lyon had won both times. But Barcelona were the ones with a title to defend this time around, and the game was played in Bilbao, Spain. This meant it was almost like a home game for Barcelona, giving them a slight advantage. But would that be enough to see them lift the trophy?

The final was a glorious occasion and one of the biggest nights in football. More than 50,000 fans filled the stadium, all screaming for their teams. Ona knew loads of her family and friends were among them, cheering for her every step of the way. But as big of a night as it was for Ona, it was even bigger for Barcelona.

It was their last game of the season and their greatest chance to win a historic quadruple.

Ona didn't get to start the game. Instead, she came on as a substitute in the 66th minute. Barcelona had gone 1-0 up through a goal from Bonmatí by then, but there was still plenty of the game left. After all, Lyon were one of the best teams in

Europe, so Ona had to be at her best to make sure Barcelona won.

Ona's best moment came deep into injury time, when she had the ball partway into Lyon's half. She was dispossessed, but the ball only went as far as Clàudia Pina. Pina passed the ball back to Ona, who controlled it and then sent Pina off down the line.

Pina entered the Lyon box, took one touch and pulled it back for Alexia Putellas. Putellas then smashed the ball into the roof of the Lyon net!

'History beckons big time for Barcelona!' screamed the commentator.

There was no way back for Lyon after that. Barcelona won the match 2-0 and lifted the Champions League trophy to claim the quadruple!

It was glorious, and the celebrations were wild, long and loud. Ona hung out on the pitch to cheer and celebrate with all the players as the fans watched on. She hopped on the podium with the team and screamed with her teammates as their captain lifted the trophy and fireworks and streamers blasted into the sky!

She had dreamt of this moment since she was a little girl and now it had come true. Not only was Ona a Champions League winner, but she was also a quadruple champion!

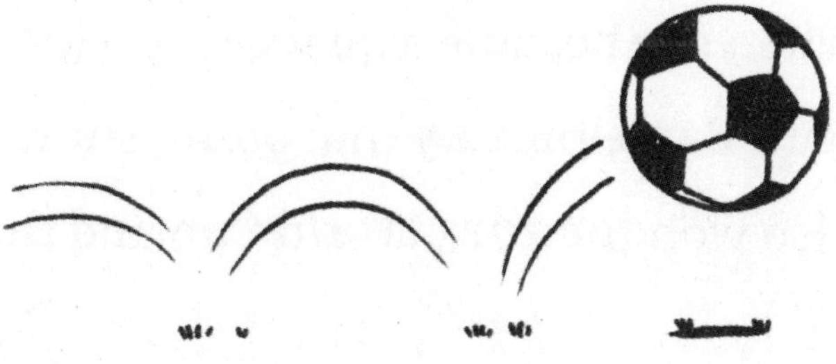

14
ONA'S FUTURE

Ona has achieved so much in her career that it's easy to forget that she was still only twenty-four years old when she became a quadruple winner with Barcelona. By that point, she'd also won the 2023 World Cup and the

2023/2024 Nations League with Spain.

On an individual level, she'd also won trophies such as the Manchester United Women's Player of the Year and the PFA WSL Fans' Player of the Year. These awards show that she is loved by football pundits and fans all over the world, making her an inspiration to all future generations.

When Ona was younger, she looked up to Dani Alves as a stunning full-back who led wicked attacks for his team. But as she grew and started playing

professionally, Ona got inspired by exciting women playing the game. She loved watching the likes of England's Lucy Bronze or Spain's Marta Torrejón. Now Ona is someone who younger players can dream about becoming too.

Everybody can see how hard Ona works to constantly improve her game. And when it comes time for her to stand up for what she believes in – such as when she and the other Spanish players stood against the

Spanish football federation – then she will do that with dignity as well. She gives her all to everything on and off the field, and people love that about her.

What is left for Ona to achieve? She wants what all good players want: to be the best in the world and win as many major tournaments as possible. The next one up for Spain is the Euro 2025, and then they aim to defend their world title at the 2027 World Cup.

'I think we're in a very good moment for women's football in Spain,' she said. 'We have to enjoy it because the best moments don't come around often, so it's about enjoying it and wanting more. I always want more, and I believe that we have a brilliant future ahead of us.'

And if Ona can keep enjoying her football, there's no telling how good things can get. 'We want to keep growing. It's just the beginning,' she said.